ABRAHAM LINCOLN'S GETTYSBURG ADDRESS

FRONT SEAT OF HISTORY: FAMOUS SPEECHES

WITHDRAWN

Fitchburg Public Library
5530 Lacy Road
Fitchburg, WI 53711

TAMRA ORR

Published in the United States of America by Cherry Lake Publishing Group
Ann Arbor, Michigan
www.cherrylakepublishing.com

Reading Adviser: Marla Conn, MS, Ed., Literacy specialist, Read-Ability, Inc.
Content Adviser: Adam Fulton Johnson, PhD, Assistant Professor, History, Philosophy, and Sociology of Science, Michigan State University
Photo credits: © Everett Historical/Shutterstock.com, cover, 5, 11, 15, 16, 19, 21, 28 [top]; 28 [bottom]; © Mathew Brady, U.S. National Archives, 111-B-358, 6; © Mathew Brady, U.S. National Archives, 111-B-264, 8; © Mathew Brady, U.S. National Archives, 111-B-486, 12; © Mathew Brady, U.S. National Archives, NWDNS-11-B-204, 14; © Bob Pool/Shutterstock.com, 22; © Tupungato/Shutterstock.com, 25; © Jack R Perry Photography/Shutterstock.com, 26; © Library of Congress, LC-USZ62-109539, 29 [top]; © Library of Congress, LC-DIG-ppmsca-19926, 29 [bottom]

Copyright ©2021 by Cherry Lake Publishing Group
All rights reserved. No part of this book may be reproduced or utilized in any form or by any means without written permission from the publisher.

Cherry Lake Press is an imprint of Cherry Lake Publishing Group.

Library of Congress Cataloging-in-Publication Data
Names: Orr, Tamra, author.
Title: Abraham Lincoln's Gettysburg Address / Tamra Orr.
Description: Ann Arbor, Michigan : Cherry Lake Publishing, 2021 | Series: Front seat of history: famous speeches | Includes index. | Audience: Grades 4-6
Identifiers: LCCN 2020005528 (print) | LCCN 2020005529 (ebook) | ISBN 9781534168787 (hardcover) | ISBN 9781534170469 (paperback) | ISBN 9781534172302 (pdf) | ISBN 9781534174146 (ebook)
Subjects: LCSH: Lincoln, Abraham, 1809-1865. Gettysburg Address—Juvenile literature. | United States—History—Civil War, 1861-1865—Causes—Juvenile literature. | Slavery—United States—Juvenile literature.
Classification: LCC E475.55 .O77 2020 (print) | LCC E475.55 (ebook) | DDC 973.7/349—dc23
LC record available at https://lccn.loc.gov/2020005528
LC ebook record available at https://lccn.loc.gov/2020005529

Cherry Lake Publishing Group would like to acknowledge the work of the Partnership for 21st Century Learning, a Network of Battelle for Kids. Please visit http://www.battelleforkids.org/networks/p21 for more information.

Printed in the United States of America
Corporate Graphics

ABOUT THE AUTHOR

Tamra Orr is the author of more than 500 nonfiction books for readers of all ages. A graduate of Ball State University, she now lives in the Pacific Northwest with her family. When she isn't writing books, she is either camping, reading or on the computer researching the latest topics.

TABLE OF CONTENTS

CHAPTER 1
A Big Sacrifice 4

CHAPTER 2
"For Us the Living" 10

CHAPTER 3
"Shall Not Have Died in Vain" 18

CHAPTER 4
Memorizing with Meaning 24

TIMELINE 28-29
SPEECH HIGHLIGHT 30
RESEARCH AND ACT 31
FURTHER READING 31
GLOSSARY 32
INDEX 32

CHAPTER 1

A Big Sacrifice

In 1861, the nation was rocked by the Civil War. Suddenly, state borders created enemies. Depending on where you lived, you either fought alongside your family or you fought against them on the battlefield. America was truly a "nation divided" over issues of slavery and basic human rights. At the time of Abraham Lincoln's famous speech at the Soldiers' National Cemetery, now the Gettysburg National Cemetery, on November 19, 1863, the country was tired and hurting from the huge loss of men on both sides of the fight. The president knew he needed to find a way to let the people know that their sacrifices were made for a good reason. He also needed them to know that the principles of liberty and equality written about in the Declaration of Independence were behind every decision he made.

Crowds gather for President Lincoln's inauguration on March 4, 1861.

Straightening her hat, Molly glanced around at the huge crowd making its way down Baltimore Street to the Soldiers' National Cemetery. She had never seen this many people in her life. The small roads were jammed with people wanting to witness the **dedication** of the new cemetery and perhaps get a look at President Lincoln.

[ABRAHAM LINCOLN'S GETTYSBURG ADDRESS]

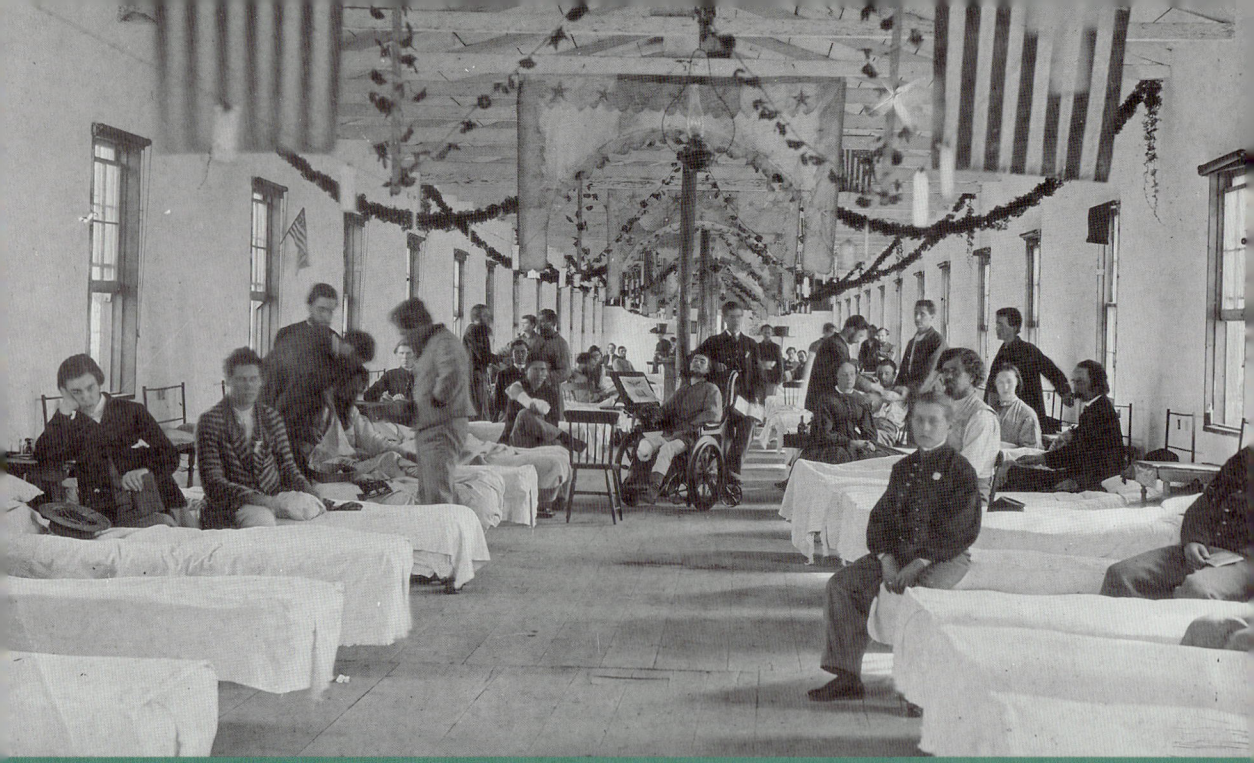
Two-thirds of the soldiers who fought in the Civil War died of infection or disease.

"Don't dawdle, Mol," said Mrs. Harrison, reaching over to tighten the bow under her daughter's chin. Her mother's face looked tense and pale. It reminded Molly that despite wearing their best Sunday clothes, this was far from a festive occasion. They were on their way to listen to speeches about the loss of many **Union** soldiers at the Battle of Gettysburg 4 months earlier. Unfortunately, one of those killed had been Molly's older brother, Thomas.

While much of the North celebrated one of its biggest victories, the Harrison family kept their doors closed and mourned. Molly couldn't believe her brother was really gone. Months later, it still did not feel real. She was sure he would stroll in through the front door at any moment and ask how soon it was until dinnertime.

When the Harrisons got to the cemetery, they found a place to stand among the thousands of other spectators. Molly felt squeezed from every direction. She could barely see the raised platform where the president would stand.

"There he is!" someone shouted. Molly stood up on her tiptoes just in time to see President Lincoln arrive on horseback. He was followed by a line of carriages and men in military uniforms. Glancing over at her parents, she saw the pain on their faces. Seeing the soldiers was a grim reminder of the big sacrifice their family had made.

Photographer Mathew Brady was able to document the Civil War.

The crowd hushed as Edward Everett stood up and walked over to the **podium**. Molly's father had told her about this man. He was a former U.S. senator and secretary of state. Molly thought he looked quite stern. He began speaking, describing the battle where so many fathers, sons, and brothers had been lost. Many people in the audience were crying.

After Everett finished his speech, a military band began playing a hymn. People began looking around. Molly stood up straighter. It was time for the president!

David Wills's Job

*Pennsylvania **attorney** David Wills knew all about the uglier side of war. In July 1863, he opened his home to soldiers wounded at Gettysburg. When the battle was over, the city was faced with thousands of fallen soldiers. Wills was given the job of making sure each person was buried properly. He worked hard, raised money, and bought 17 acres (7 hectares) of land that would become the Gettysburg National Cemetery.*

[ABRAHAM LINCOLN'S GETTYSBURG ADDRESS]

CHAPTER 2

"For Us the Living"

"**O**h my!" Molly gasped as President Abraham Lincoln walked up to the podium. The man was every bit as tall as she had been told. His height, long black suit, and **stovepipe hat** made him seem like a giant, even from where Molly stood in the crowd.

"**Fourscore** and seven years ago," the president began, "our fathers brought forth on this continent a new nation, conceived in liberty and dedicated to the **proposition** that all men are created equal."

Molly immediately recognized that the president was referring to the country's Declaration of Independence and its focus on "equality for all."

Abraham Lincoln was America's tallest president.

Cannons and other artillery played an important role in the Civil War.

Gesturing toward the cemetery, Lincoln continued, "We have come to dedicate a portion of that field as a final resting place for those who here gave their lives that that nation might live. It is altogether fitting and proper that we should do this. But, in a larger sense, we cannot dedicate, we cannot **consecrate**, we cannot **hallow** this ground."

"What does he mean, Robert?" Mrs. Harrison whispered to her husband. He shook his head. Molly looked around and saw confusion on many people's faces.

"The brave men, living and dead, who struggled here have consecrated it far above our poor power to add or detract," Lincoln explained.

During the Civil War, soldiers spent the majority of their time at camp.

Now people were nodding. Molly saw her parents clasp hands. They knew Lincoln was referring to their son, among the many who had been lost.

"The world will little note nor long remember what we say here, but it can never forget what they did here. It is for us the living, rather, to be dedicated here to the unfinished work which they who fought here have thus far so nobly advanced," said the president.

African Americans fought for the Union during the Civil War.

Artists made paintings of Lincoln's speech.

He is challenging us again, thought Molly. *He is saying we cannot forget what all of these men, like Thomas, were fighting for. And it is up to us to keep the fight going.* Looking around at people's faces, Molly was not sure if they were able to do that. The losses were so deep and painful. Would the nation unite and survive this Civil War?

Remembered, but Not Recorded

The speeches at Gettysburg were held long before there were microphones. So it is unlikely that anyone beyond the first rows could have heard the speakers very well. No recordings were made that day either. While pictures of Edward Everett and others were taken, Lincoln's speech was over so quickly that there are no photographs of him actually speaking!

"Shall Not Have Died in Vain"

"For us—the living?" someone behind Molly said indignantly. "Exactly what does Lincoln expect us to do? Haven't we given enough, lost enough to this war?"

President Abraham Lincoln's following words answered those questions. "It is rather for us to be here dedicated to the great task remaining before us—that from these honored dead we take increased devotion to that cause for which they gave the last full measure of devotion," he stated. "That we here highly resolve that these dead shall not have died in vain."

Mrs. Harrison bowed her head, and Molly knew that she was thinking of Thomas. Losing him was hard. But if it had

President Lincoln issued the **Emancipation** Proclamation in 1863, which freed all slaves if the Union won the Civil War.

been for nothing—if their sacrifice meant nothing—that would be too much to bear.

"That this nation, under God, shall have a new birth of freedom; and that government of the people, by the people, for the people shall not perish from the earth," Lincoln said.

Then, to the astonishment of the thousands of people standing there, he left the podium.

A shocked silence filled the air before polite applause rippled across the crowd. Louder was the murmur of voices who couldn't believe the president could possibly be finished. The entire speech had lasted only 2 minutes!

"He's done?" Mr. Harrison asked in surprise.

"Already?" asked Molly. She had never, ever seen such a short speech. It had been different from Mr. Edward Everett's speech in every way. Not only was it a mere fraction of the length, but Everett's words had been aggressive. He talked of victory and battle. Lincoln's words had been of honor. They were about the importance of continuing to fight for the ideals that the Declaration of Independence spoke of years ago. His speech didn't need flowery vocabulary or graphic details to be powerful. The emotion was strong enough all on its own.

"I heard that Lincoln was a last-minute addition to the ceremony," someone in the crowd said. "He probably had to write that speech on the train on the way here."

President Lincoln strategized with General George B. McClellan during the Civil War.

An estimated 620,000 men died during the Civil War.

As Molly headed back home with her parents, she could hear them talking about the speech. Her father found it disappointing. "It was too short to say much of anything," he complained. "He should have been better prepared. I can't say I feel any better about this war."

Mrs. Harrison disagreed. "He was brief but so heartfelt," she said. "I don't know if I will ever forget his words. I want to believe him—to believe that Thomas did not give his life in vain."

The following day, the newspapers were full of stories about the speeches at Gettysburg. Some reports shared Mr. Harrison's thoughts, **criticizing** President Lincoln and calling his words "silly" and "**flat**." Other reports praised the speech, calling it "**elegant**" and "sincere."

When the Civil War ended in 1865, the North won. President Lincoln's words about a "government of the people, by the people, for the people" came true. Tragically, less than a week later, he was **assassinated**.

Gettysburg National Cemetery

More than 3,500 Union soldiers were buried in Gettysburg. Of those, almost 1,000 were buried in unmarked graves, since there was no way to identify them. Because this cemetery is now part of a national park, soldiers from other periods in history are also buried there, including World War II and the Korean War.

Memorizing with Meaning

"Fourscore and seven years ago," Jeremy rehearsed, staring straight ahead so he couldn't check his notes, "our fathers brought forth on this continent a new nation, conceived in liberty and dedicated to the prop...the prep...the...what is it again?" He sighed with frustration and looked down at the copy of the speech. He had been working to memorize this speech for 3 days. Even though it was less than 300 words long, he was still making mistakes.

"How is it going?" Jeremy's dad asked, popping his head into the bedroom. The look on his son's face was all the answer he needed. "Can I ask you a question? Do you have any idea why Lincoln gave this speech in the first place?"

Approximately 6 million people visit the Lincoln Memorial each year.

Jeremy sheepishly shook his head. He had chosen the Gettysburg Address because it was the shortest famous speech he could find.

"When Lincoln made that speech, the country was divided into two sides, often pitting families against each other," his dad explained. "People were angry and scared. They worried the war would hurt the nation instead of unite it. Lincoln's speech was made to encourage

Abraham Lincoln's speech was only 272 words.

those who doubted. He was explaining to Americans that they had to dedicate themselves to creating an equal and fair land, just like the people who 'fourscore and seven years' earlier had written the Declaration of Independence."

"Oh," Jeremy realized. So that's what that phrase meant!

For the next hour, Jeremy and his dad researched even more about Lincoln and the Gettysburg Address. He imagined being in the crowd, listening to the president deliver this brief but important message.

The next afternoon at school, Jeremy finished reciting with Lincoln's words "and that government of the people, by the people, for the people shall not perish from the earth." When he was done, he was proud. And he was grateful that his performance got more than just a little polite applause like Lincoln had received.

Reflecting on Lincoln's Words

A copy of the Gettysburg Address is kept in the White House's Lincoln Bedroom. In 2013, President Barack Obama reflected on that speech: "This **quintessentially** self-made man, fierce in his belief in honest work and the striving spirit at the heart of America, believed that it falls to each generation, collectively, to share in that toil and sacrifice. Through cold war and world war, through industrial revolution and technological transformation, through movements for civil rights and women's rights and workers' rights and gay rights, we have. At times, social and economic changes have strained our union. But Lincoln's words give us confidence that whatever trials await us, this nation and the freedoms we cherish can, and shall, **prevail**."

TIMELINE

1860
Abraham Lincoln is elected 16th president of the United States.

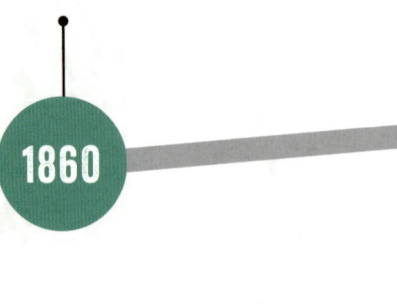

1861
The Civil War begins.

28 [21ST CENTURY SKILLS LIBRARY]

1863
Lincoln signs the Emancipation Proclamation.

1865
The Civil War ends; Lincoln is assassinated.

1863

1864

1865

1863
Lincoln delivers the Gettysburg Address.

1864
Lincoln is reelected president.

[ABRAHAM LINCOLN'S GETTYSBURG ADDRESS]   29

Speech Highlight

"It is rather for us to be here dedicated to the great task remaining before us—that from these honored dead we take increased devotion to that cause for which they gave the last full measure of devotion; that we here highly resolve that these dead shall not have died in vain; that this nation, under God, shall have a new birth of freedom; and that government of the people, by the people, for the people shall not perish from the earth."

Read the full speech at https://voicesofdemocracy.umd.edu/lincoln-gettysburg-address-speech-text.

Research and Act

Abraham Lincoln was known for many things, including fighting against slavery, being a strong debater, and giving some very powerful speeches on important issues.

Research
In the years since Lincoln's death, his Gettysburg Address has been recorded and recited by many people, including Johnny Cash and Bill Clinton. Research different versions of the Gettysburg Address online and see who you believe does the best job.

Act
Memorize one paragraph of the Gettysburg Address and perform it for family or friends. Get their thoughts on what they think it meant and share with them what you have learned.

Further Reading

Kanefield, Teri. *Abraham Lincoln.* New York, NY: Abrams Books for Young Readers, 2018.

O'Connor, Jim. *What Was the Battle of Gettysburg?* New York, NY: Grosset and Dunlap, 2013.

Olson, Kay Melchisedech. *The Gettysburg Address in Translation: What It Really Means.* North Mankato, MN: Capstone Press, 2018.

Vansant, Wayne. *Gettysburg: The Graphic History of America's Most Famous Battle and the Turning Point of the Civil War.* Minneapolis, MN: Zenith Press, 2013.

GLOSSARY

assassinated (uh-SAS-uh-nay-tid) murdered for political reasons

attorney (uh-TUR-nee) a person who practices law; a lawyer

consecrate (KAHN-suh-krate) to make or declare something as sacred

criticizing (KRIT-ih-size-ing) telling what someone has done wrong

dedication (ded-ih-KAY-shuhn) a special ceremony held to mark the opening of something new

elegant (EL-uh-guhnt) high quality, neat, and simple

emancipation (ih-man-suh-PAY-shuhn) freedom

flat (FLAT) dull, boring, shallow

fourscore (FOR-skor) 4 times 20, or 80

hallow (HAL-oh) to make holy

podium (POH-dee-uhm) a stand with a surface for holding papers, for use by a person giving a speech

prevail (prih-VAYL) to triumph: to succeed

proposition (prah-puh-ZISH-uhn) an idea or course of action suggested

quintessentially (kwin-tuh-SEN-shuhl-ee) to be the perfect example of something

stovepipe hat (STOHV-pipe HAT) a tall top hat popular in the 1800s

Union (YOON-yuhn) the Northern states that supported the end of slavery and were loyal to the federal government during the Civil War

INDEX

African Americans, 15

Battle of Gettysburg, 6, 9
Brady, Matthew, 8

Civil War, 4, 6, 8, 12, 14, 15, 19, 21, 29
  deaths, 6, 9, 22

Declaration of Independence, 4, 10, 20, 26

Emancipation Proclamation, 19, 29
equality, 4, 10
Everett, Edward, 9, 17, 20

Gettysburg Address, 10–19, 29, 30
  reason for, 25–26
Gettysburg National Cemetery, 4, 9, 10–19, 23

human rights, 4

liberty, 4
Lincoln, Abraham, 4
  assassination of, 23, 29
  Gettysburg Address, 10–19, 29, 30
  timeline, 28–29
Lincoln Memorial, 25

McClellan, George B., 21

Obama, Barack, 27

slaves/slavery, 4, 19
soldiers, 6, 9, 14, 15
  buried at Gettysburg, 23
Soldiers' National Cemetery, 4, 5–7

timeline, 28–29

Union, 6, 15, 19
  soldiers buried at Gettysburg, 23

Wills, David, 9